HAL•LEONARD® GUITAR PLAY-ALONG

AUDIO ACCESS INCLUDED

SCORPIONS

VOL. 174

PLAYBACK+

Speed • Pitch • Balance • Loop

To access audio visit:
www.halleonard.com/mylibrary

Enter Code
2549-6522-0320-7329

Photo courtesy of Michael Ochs Archives/Stringer

ISBN 978-1-4803-5415-9

HAL•LEONARD®

7777 W. BLUEMOUND RD. P.O. BOX 13819 MILWAUKEE, WI 53213

CONTENTS

Page   Title

6   Big City Nights

15   Blackout

26   No One Like You

74   Rock You Like a Hurricane

34   Sails of Charon

46   Still Loving You

56   Wind of Change

66   The Zoo

Guitar Notation Legend

THE MUSICAL STAFF shows pitches and rhythms and is divided by bar lines into measures. Pitches are named after the first seven letters of the alphabet.

TABLATURE graphically represents the guitar fingerboard. Each horizontal line represents a string, and each number represents a fret.

4th string, 2nd fret   1st & 2nd strings open, played together   open D chord

HALF-STEP BEND: Strike the note and bend up 1/2 step.

WHOLE-STEP BEND: Strike the note and bend up one step.

GRACE NOTE BEND: Strike the note and immediately bend up as indicated.

SLIGHT (MICROTONE) BEND: Strike the note and bend up 1/4 step.

BEND AND RELEASE: Strike the note and bend up as indicated, then release back to the original note. Only the first note is struck.

PRE-BEND: Bend the note as indicated, then strike it.

VIBRATO: The string is vibrated by rapidly bending and releasing the note with the fretting hand.

PALM MUTING: The note is partially muted by the pick hand lightly touching the string(s) just before the bridge.

HAMMER-ON: Strike the first (lower) note with one finger, then sound the higher note (on the same string) with another finger by fretting it without picking.

PULL-OFF: Place both fingers on the notes to be sounded. Strike the first note and without picking, pull the finger off to sound the second (lower) note.

LEGATO SLIDE: Strike the first note and then slide the same fret-hand finger up or down to the second note. The second note is not struck.

SHIFT SLIDE: Same as legato slide, except the second note is struck.

TRILL: Very rapidly alternate between the notes indicated by continuously hammering on and pulling off.

TAPPING: Hammer ("tap") the fret indicated with the pick-hand index or middle finger and pull off to the note fretted by the fret hand.

NATURAL HARMONIC: Strike the note while the fret-hand lightly touches the string directly over the fret indicated.

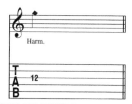

PINCH HARMONIC: The note is fretted normally and a harmonic is produced by adding the edge of the thumb or the tip of the index finger of the pick hand to the normal pick attack.

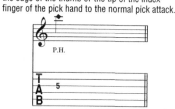

TREMOLO PICKING: The note is picked as rapidly and continuously as possible.

VIBRATO BAR DIVE AND RETURN: The pitch of the note or chord is dropped a specified number of steps (in rhythm), then returned to the original pitch.

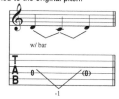

VIBRATO BAR SCOOP: Depress the bar just before striking the note, then quickly release the bar.

VIBRATO BAR DIP: Strike the note and then immediately drop a specified number of steps, then release back to the original pitch.

Additional Musical Definitions

 (accent)   • Accentuate note (play it louder).

 (staccato)   • Play the note short.

D.S. al Coda   • Go back to the sign (%), then play until the measure marked "*To Coda*," then skip to the section labelled "**Coda**."

D.C. al Fine   • Go back to the beginning of the song and play until the measure marked "*Fine*" (end).

Fill   • Label used to identify a brief melodic figure which is to be inserted into the arrangement.

N.C.   • Harmony is implied.

   • Repeat measures between signs.

• When a repeated section has different endings, play the first ending only the first time and the second ending only the second time.

Big City Nights

Words and Music by Rudolf Schenker and Klaus Meine

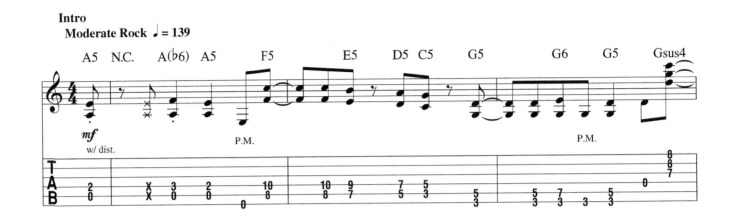

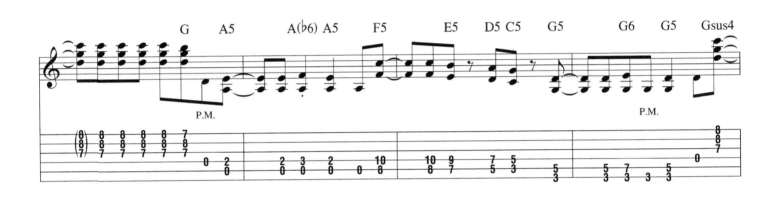

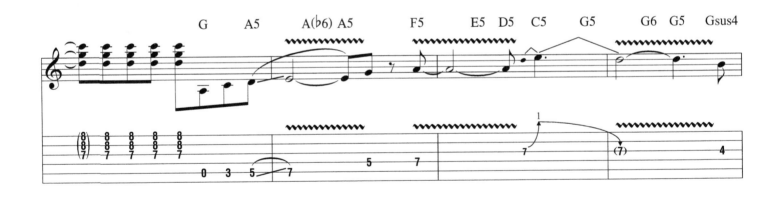

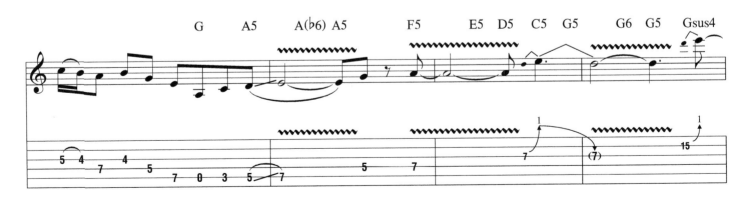

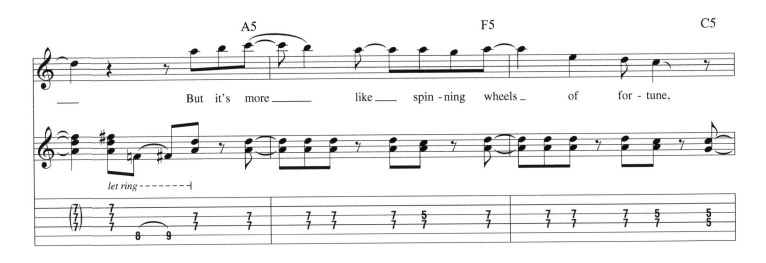

But it's more ____ like ____ spin - ning wheels ____ of for - tune,

let ring - - - - - - - ┤

which nev - er stand still. ____

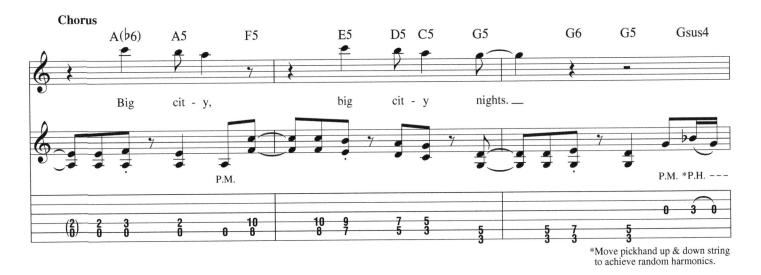

Chorus

Big cit - y, big cit - y nights. ____

P.M.

P.M. *P.H. - - -

*Move pickhand up & down string
to achieve random harmonics.

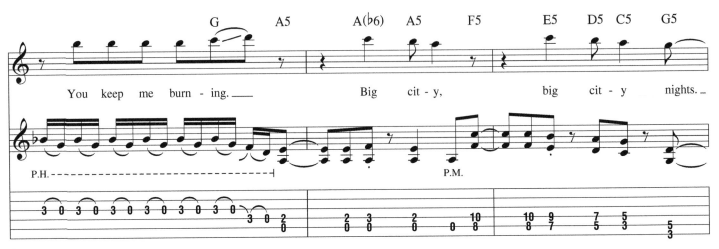

You keep me burn - ing. ____ Big cit - y, big cit - y nights. ____

P.H. - ┤

P.M.

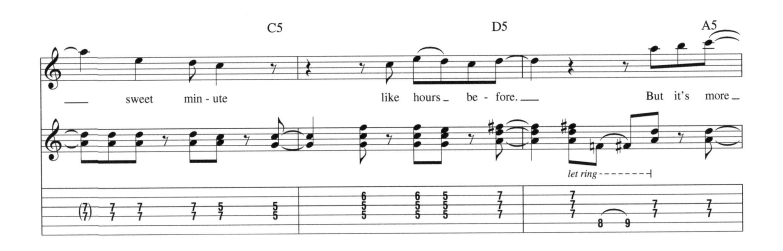

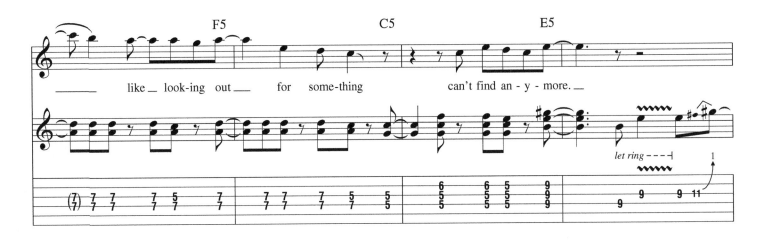

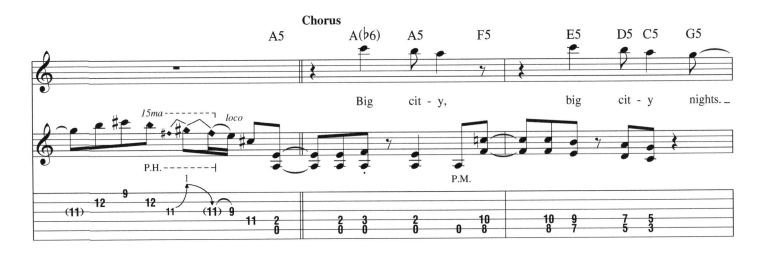

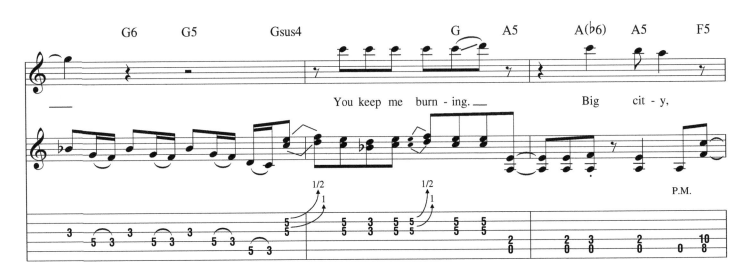

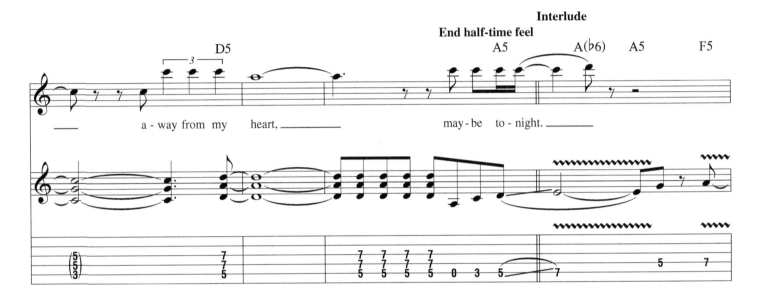

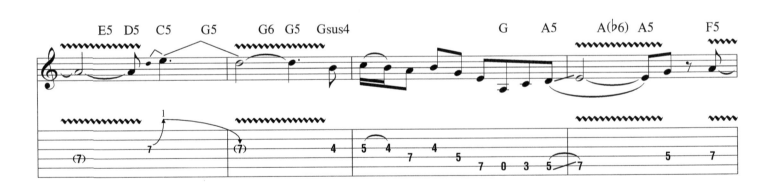

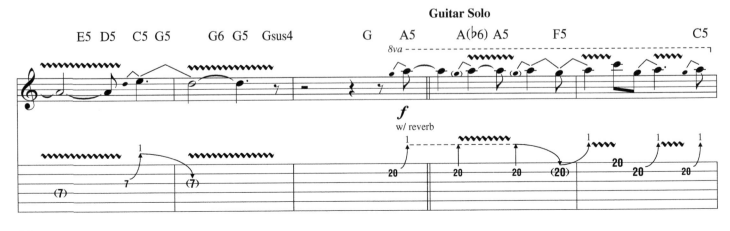

Outro-Chorus

Repeat and fade

14

Blackout

Words and Music by Rudolf Schenker, Klaus Meine, Herman Rarebell and Sonja Kittelsen

Pre-Chorus

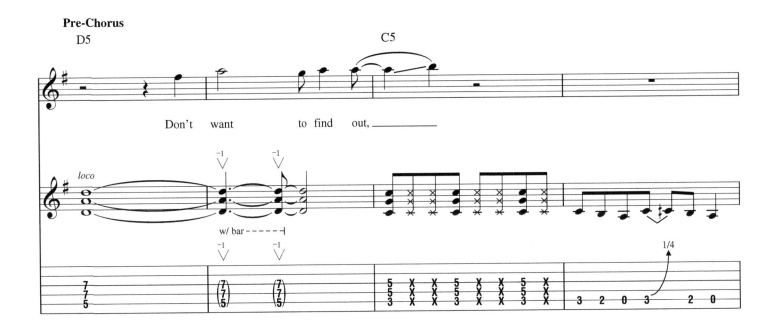

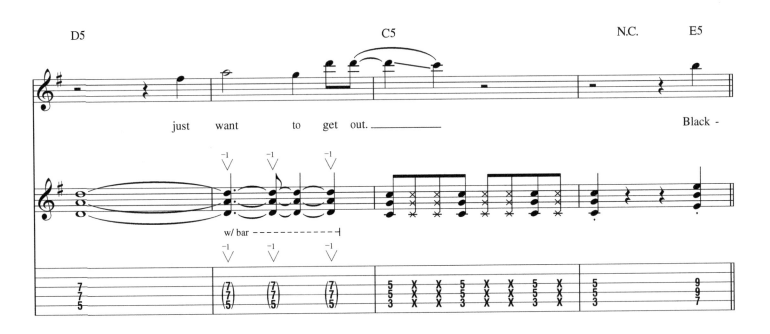

Chorus

Interlude

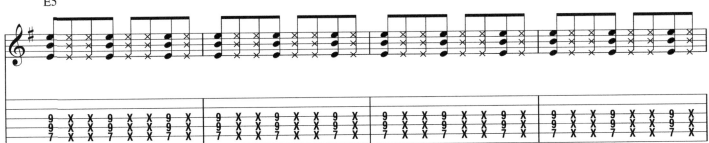

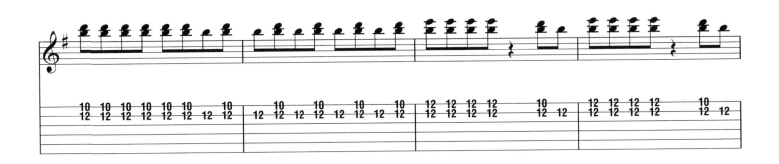

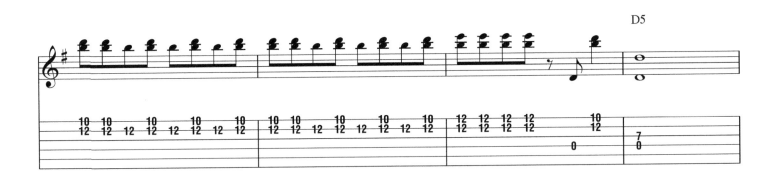

D.S. al Coda

Coda

Guitar Solo

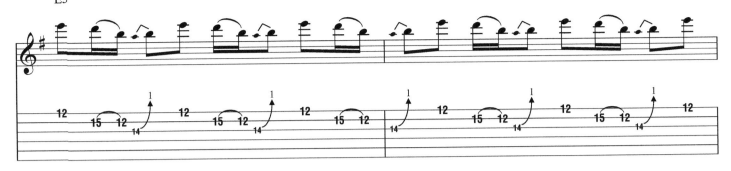

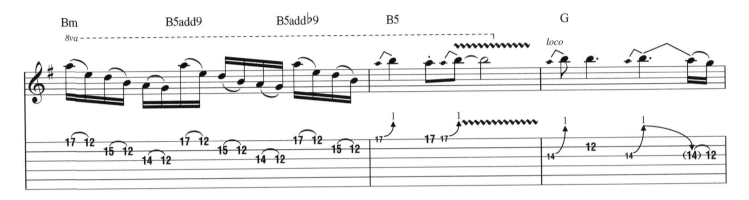

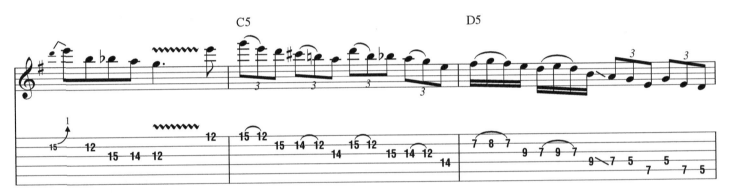

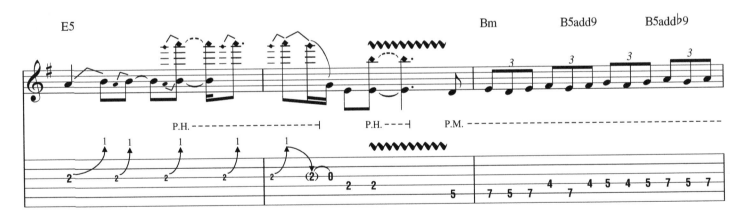

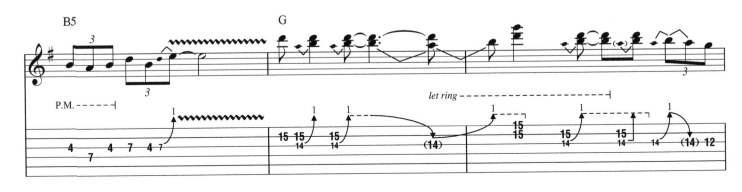

Additional Lyrics

3. I grab my things and make my run,
   On the way out, another one.
   Would like to know before I stop,
   Did I make it, or did I flop?

No One Like You

Words and Music by Rudolf Schenker and Klaus Meine

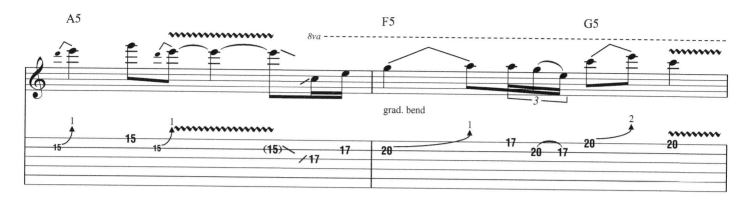

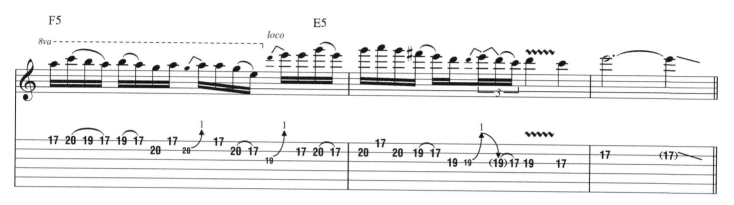

𝄋 Verse

1. Girl, been a long ___ time that we've ___ been a - part, ___ much too long ___
2. *See additional lyrics*

w/ clean tone
let chords ring throughout

___ for a man ___ who needs love. ___ I miss ___ you since I've been a -

way. _____ Babe, was-n't eas - y to leave _ you a - lone. _

w/ dist.

_ It's get - ting hard - er now _ that I'm gone; _____ if I _

_ had the choice I would stay. _____ There's no one like

I just wan - na be loved ___ by you. ___

⊕ Coda

No one like you! ___ I can't wait ___

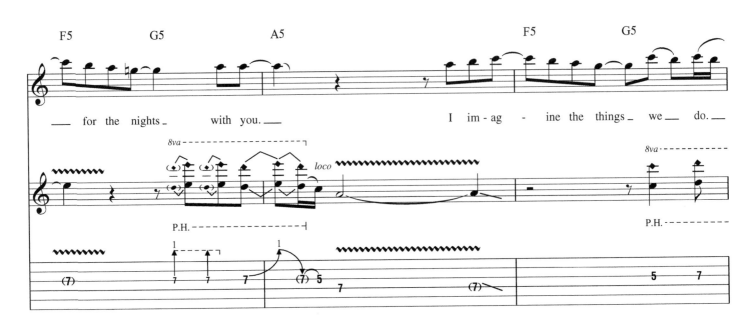

___ for the nights ___ with you. ___ I im - ag - ine the things ___ we ___ do. ___

I just wan - na be loved _ by you. _____

Guitar Solo

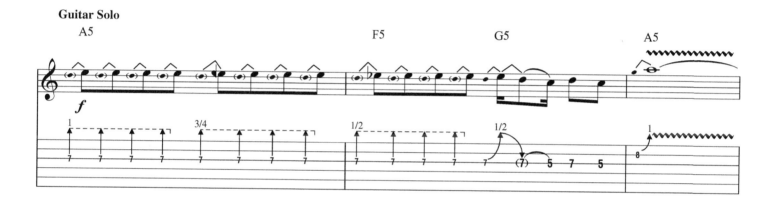

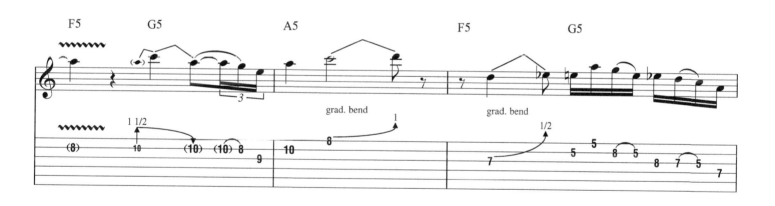

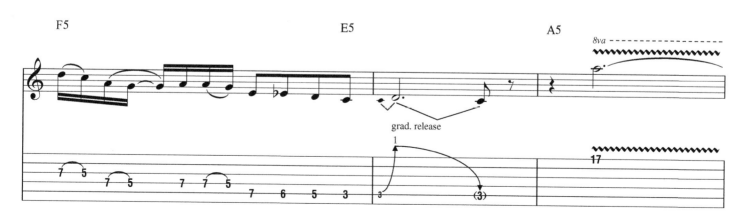

Additional Lyrics

2. Girl, there are really no words strong enough
   To describe all my longing for love.
   I don't want my feelings restrained.
   Oo, babe, I just need you like never before.
   Just imagine you'd come through this door;
   You'd take all my sorrow away.

Sails of Charon

Words and Music by Uli Roth

Tune down 1/2 step:
(low to high) E♭-A♭-D♭-G♭-B♭-E♭

Intro
Moderately ♩ = 108

*Key signature denotes C Phrygian.

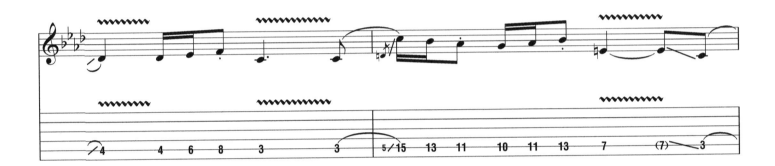

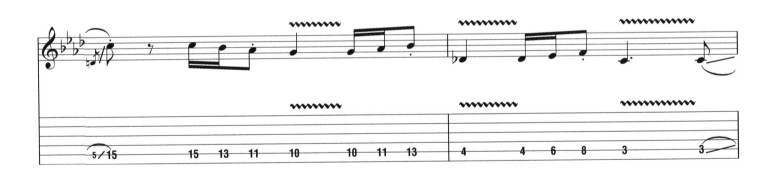

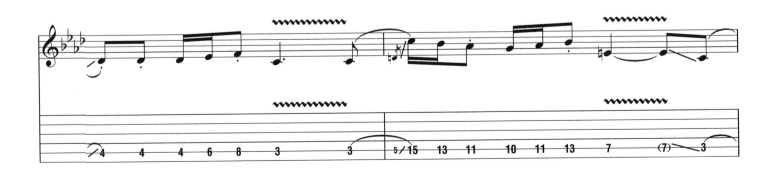

Guitar Solo

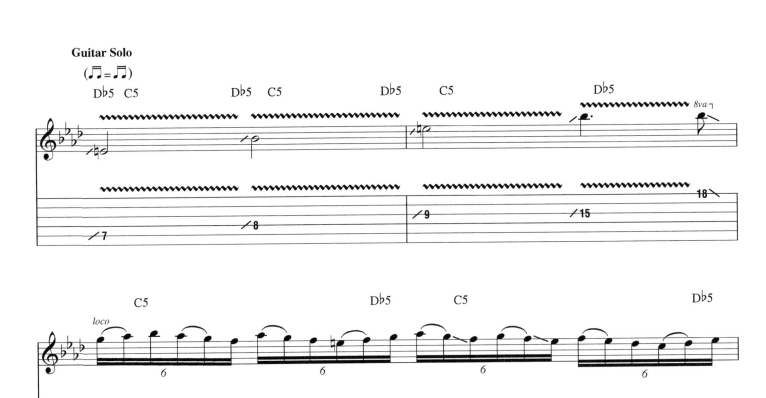

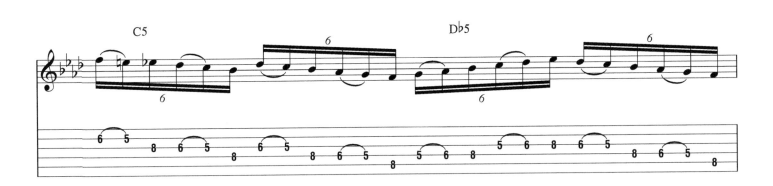

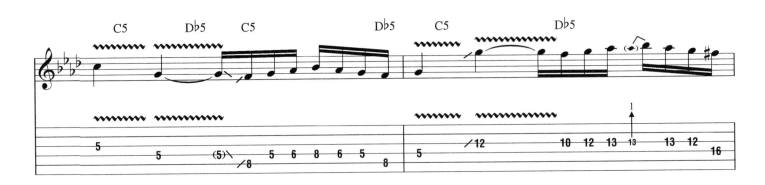

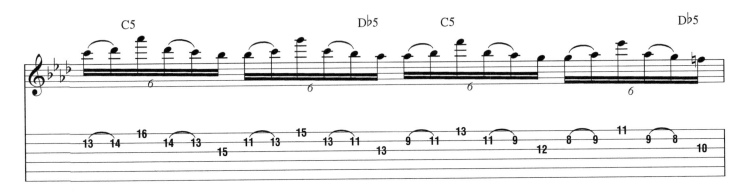

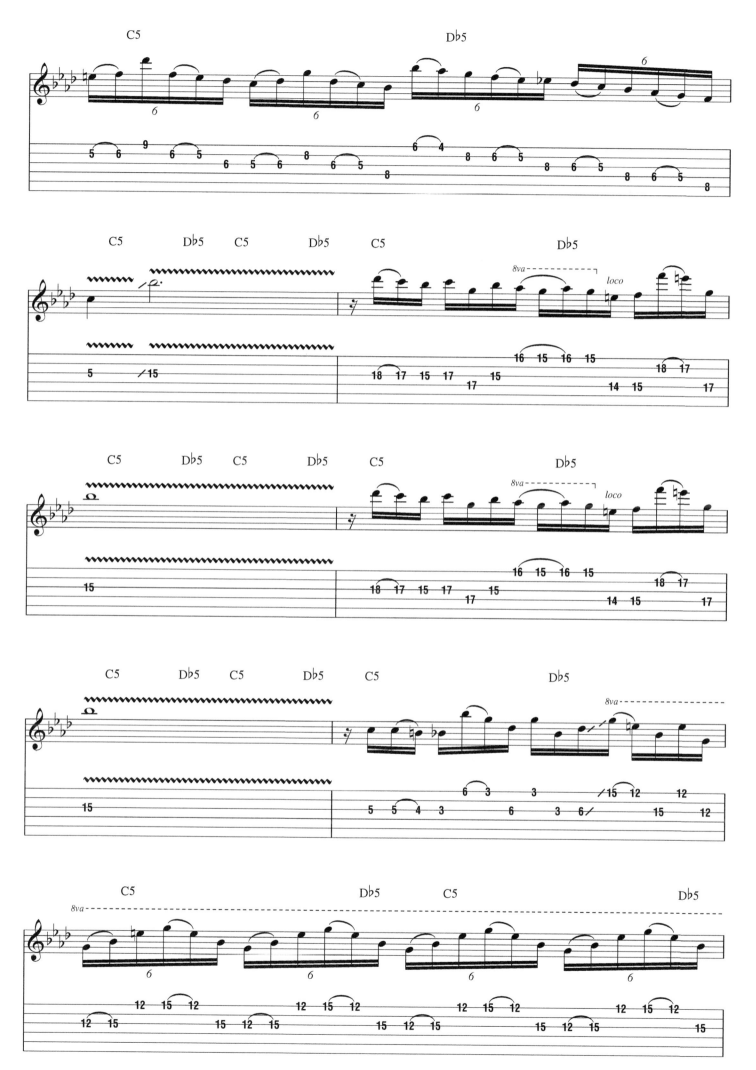

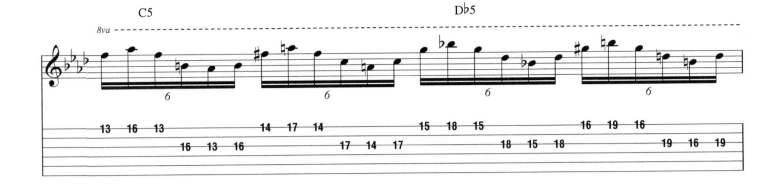

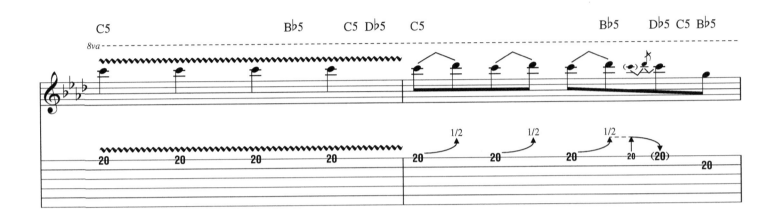

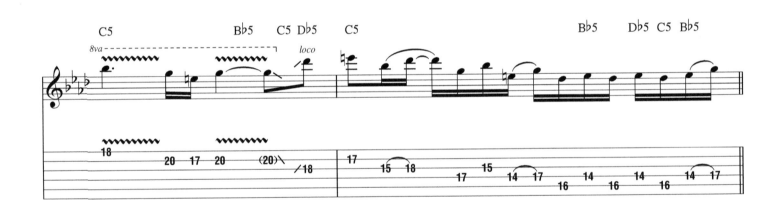

Verse

1. Dark night, _ there is no light _ in the realm ____ of the black mag-ic

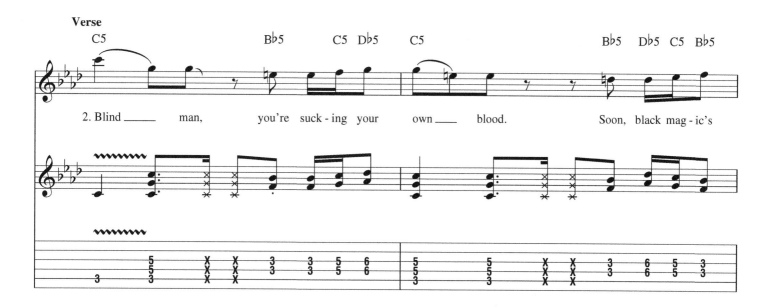

Verse

C5   Bb5   C5   Db5   C5   Bb5   Db5   C5   Bb5

2. Blind _____ man,   you're suck - ing your own _____ blood.   Soon, black mag - ic's

C5   Bb5   C5   Db5   N.C.

dy - ing.   You'd bet - ter start _____ cry - ing. _____

Interlude

Db   C   Db   C   Db

Ah. _____   Ah. _____

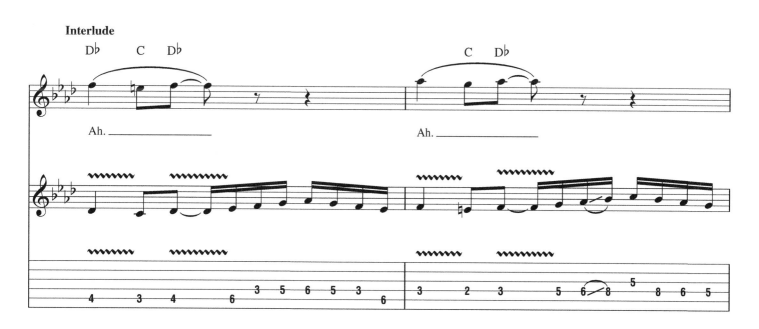

Outro

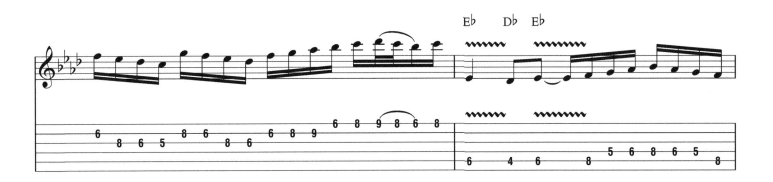

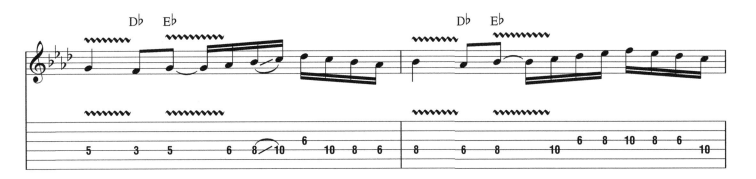

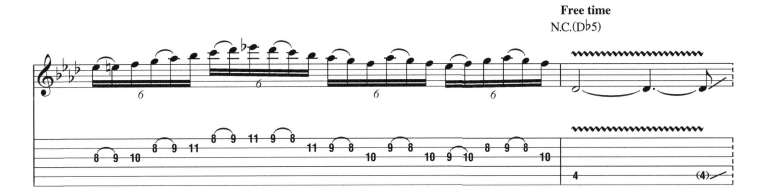

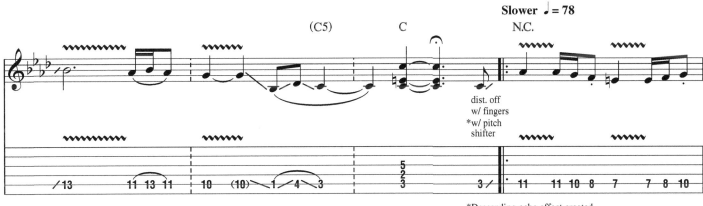

*Descending echo effect created
via detune w/ feedback.

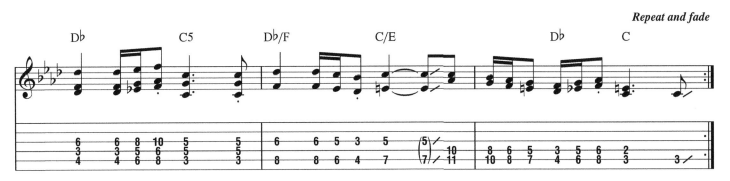

Still Loving You

Words and Music by Rudolf Schenker and Klaus Meine

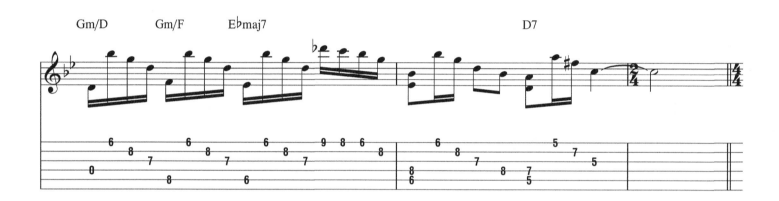

there,   I will be there.

Love,   on-ly love,   can bring back your love __ some- day.   I will __ be

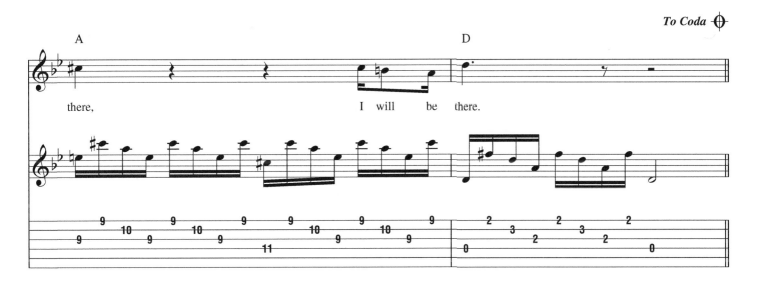

there,   I will be there.

Interlude

grad. bend

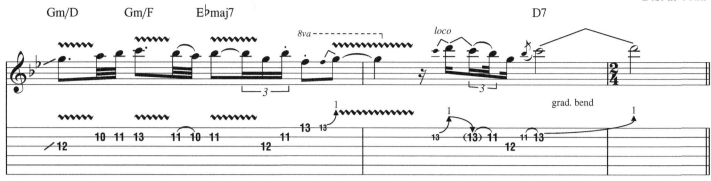

Coda

Chorus

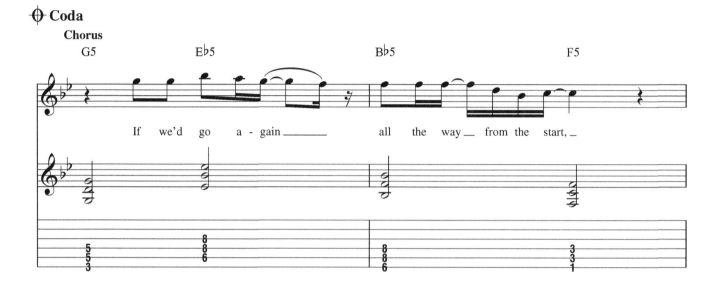

If we'd go a-gain _____ all the way __ from the start, __

I would try to change _____ things that killed our __ love. __

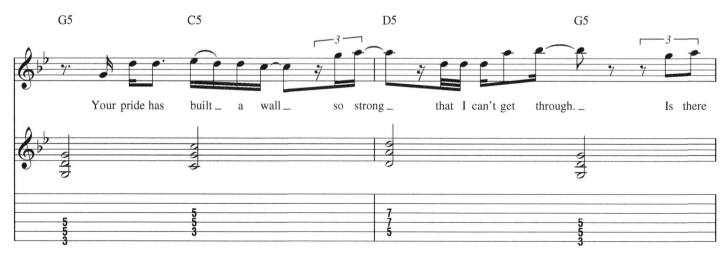

Your pride has built __ a wall __ so strong __ that I can't get through. __ Is there

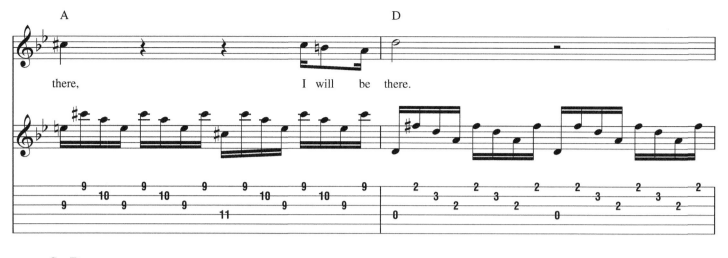

there, I will be there.

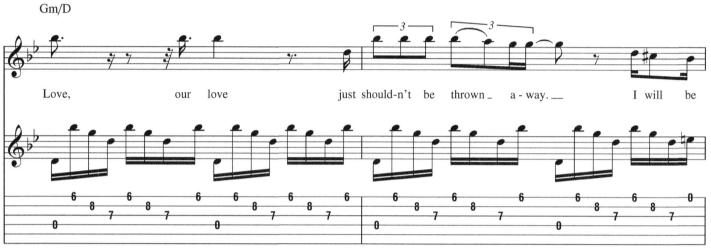

Love, our love just should-n't be thrown _ a - way. _ I will be

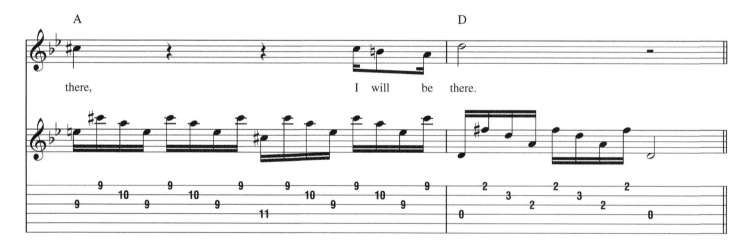

there, I will be there.

Chorus

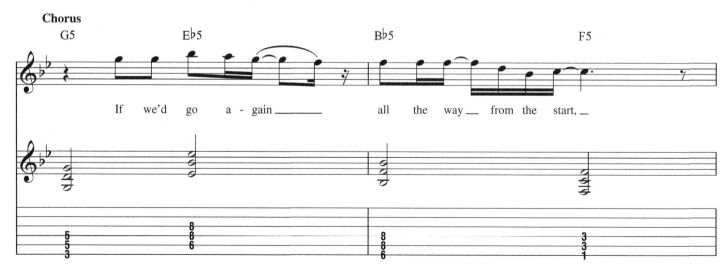

If we'd go a - gain _____ all the way _ from the start, _

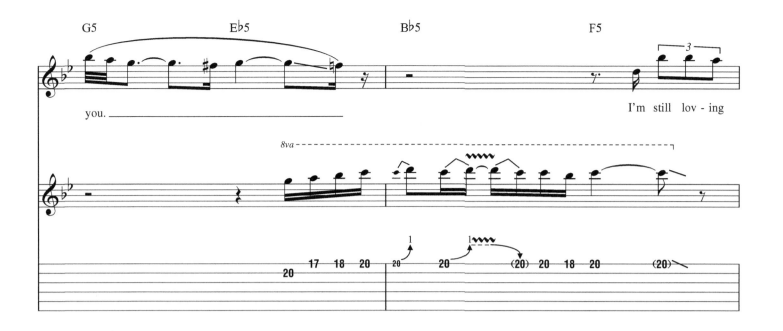

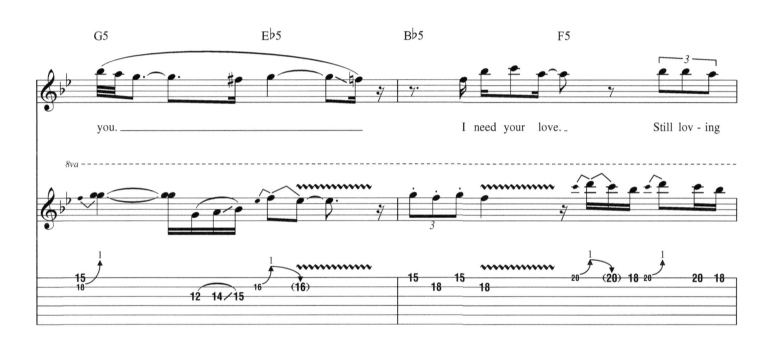

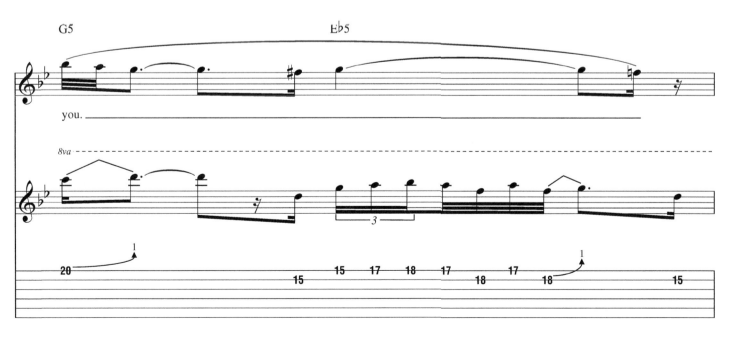

Still lov - in' you__ ba - by.   Whew!

Guitar Solo

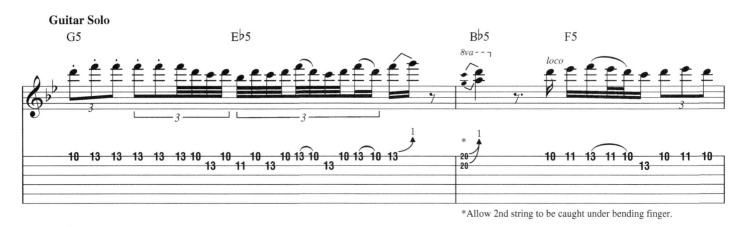

*Allow 2nd string to be caught under bending finger.

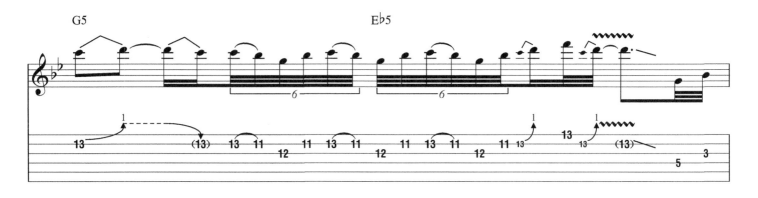

Still   lov - ing

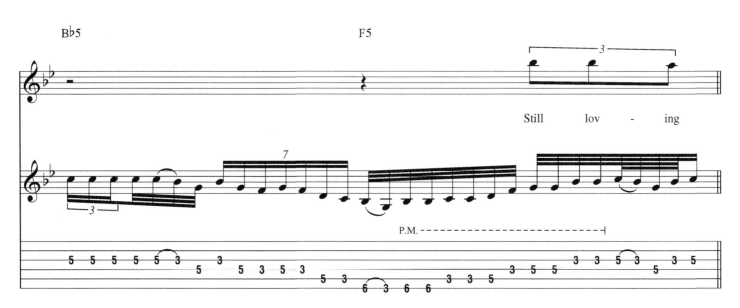

Outro-Chorus

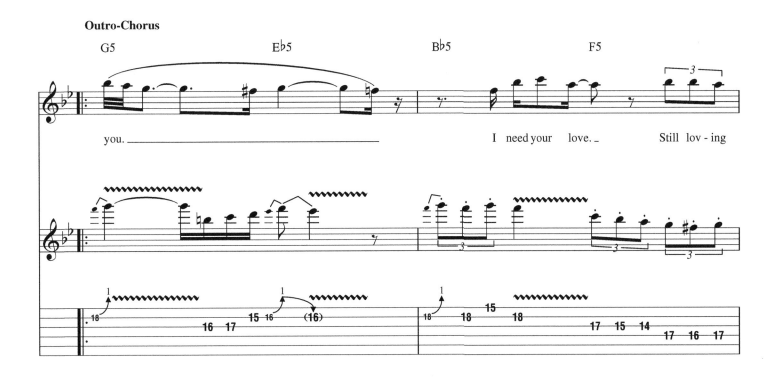

you. _____   I need your love. _   Still lov - ing

Repeat and fade

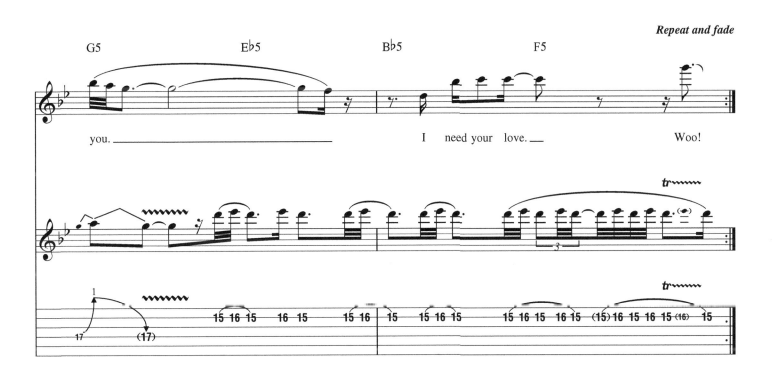

you. _____   I need your love. __   Woo!

Additional Lyrics

2. Fight, baby, fight to win back your love again.
   I will be there, I will be there.
   Love, only love can break down the wall someday.
   I will be there, I will be there.

Wind of Change

Words and Music by Klaus Meine

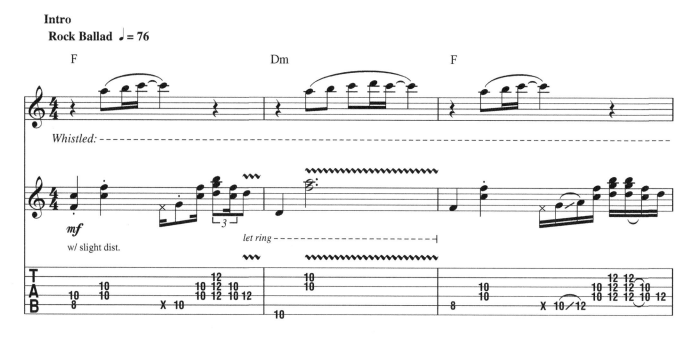

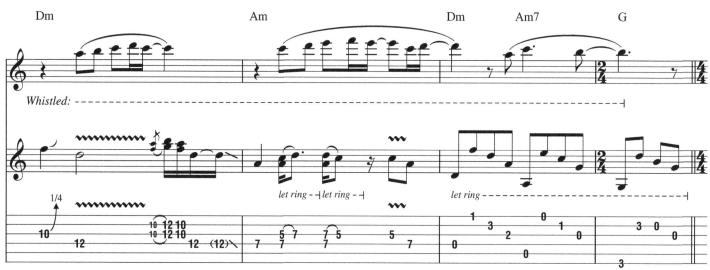

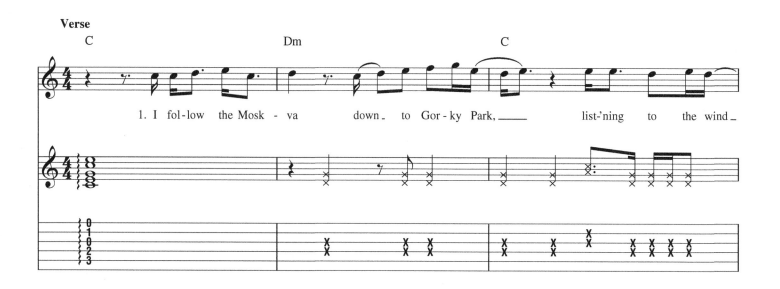

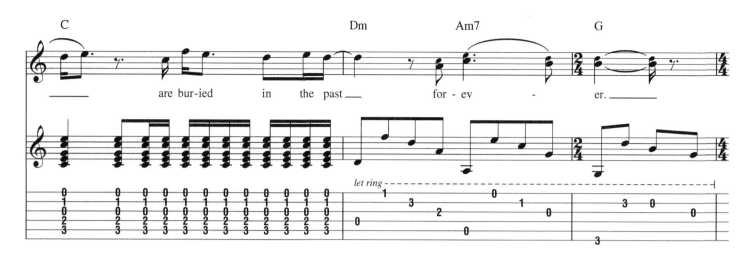

are bur-ied in the past ____ for - ev - er. ____

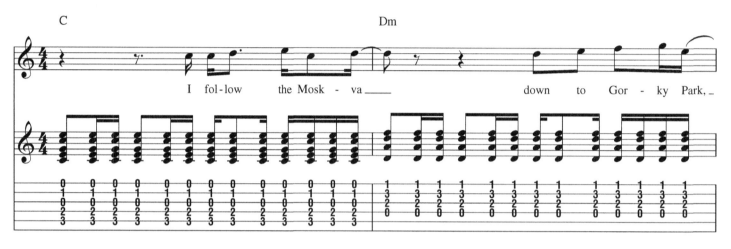

I fol-low the Mosk - va ____ down to Gor - ky Park, __

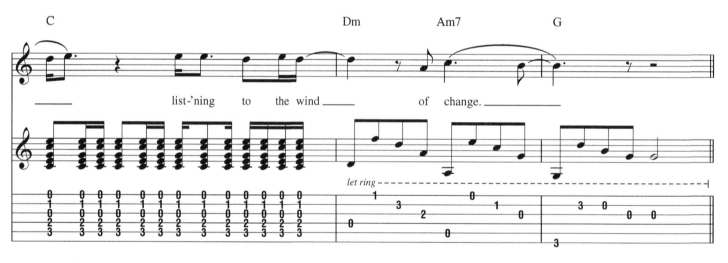

list-'ning to the wind ____ of change. ____

Chorus

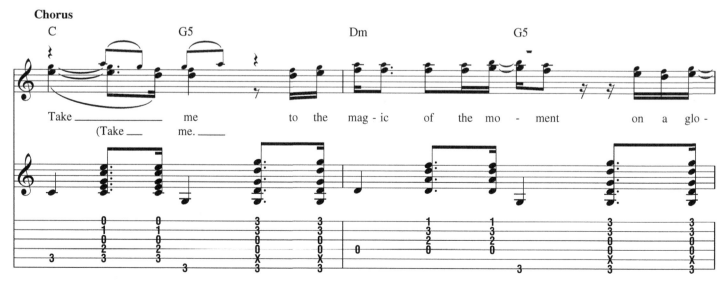

Take _____ me to the mag - ic of the mo - ment on a glo -
(Take __ me. ____)

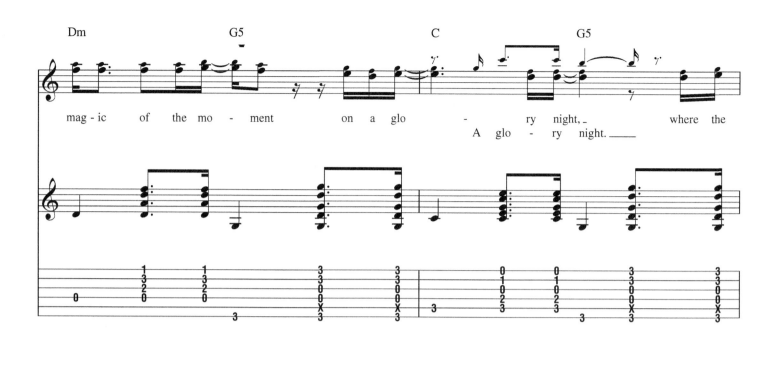

mag - ic of the mo - ment on a glo - ry night, ___ where the
A glo - ry night. ___

chil-dren of to-mor - row share their dreams ___ with you and me. ___
With you and me. __

let ring -

Take ___ me to the mag - ic of the mo - ment on a glo - ry night, ___ where the
Take me. ___ A glo - ry night. __

The Zoo

Words and Music by Rudolf Schenker and Klaus Meine

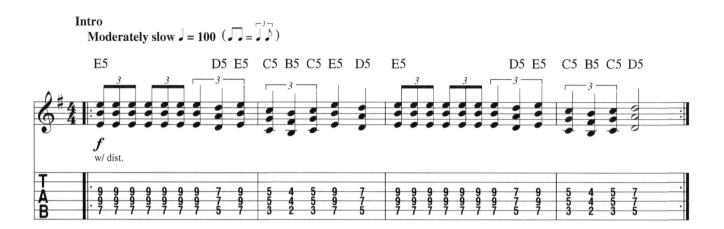

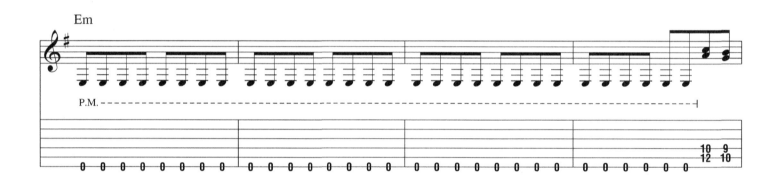

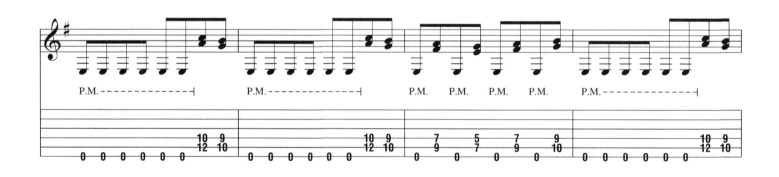

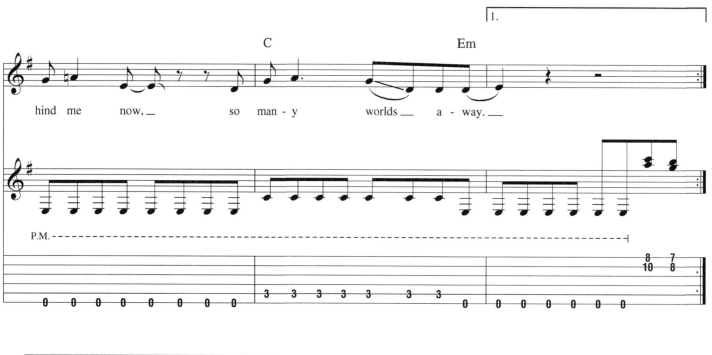

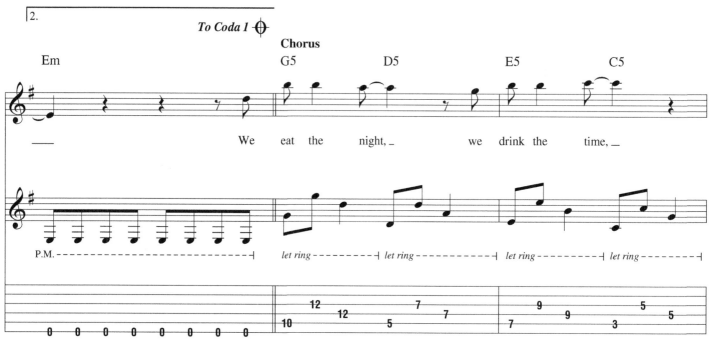

pass - ing   by ___   on streets we   call   The Zoo. ___   We

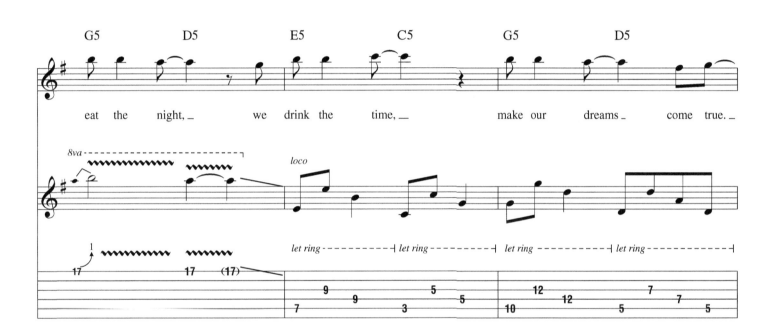

eat the   night, ___   we drink the   time, ___   make our   dreams _   come true. _

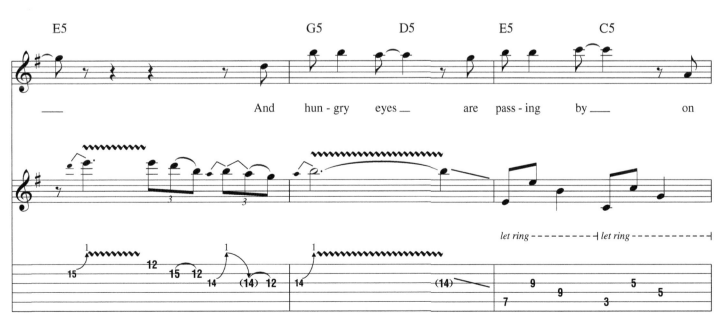

___   And hun - gry eyes ___   are pass - ing   by ___   on

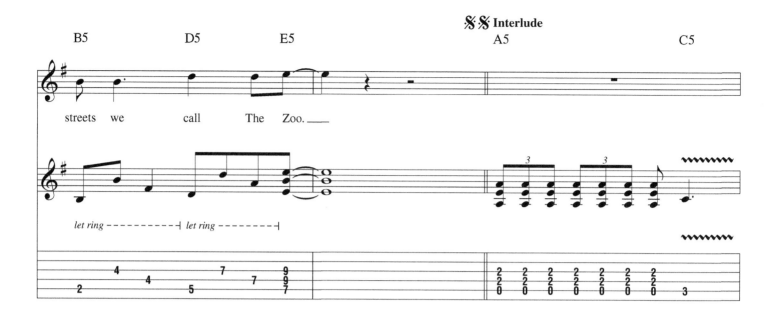

streets   we   call   The   Zoo.____

let ring --------- | let ring ---------

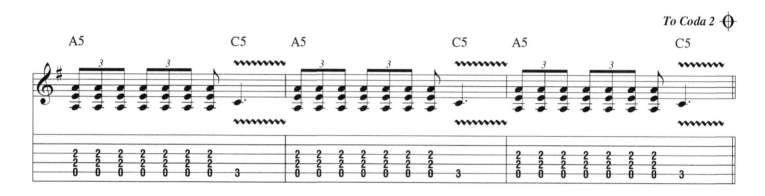

Guitar Solo

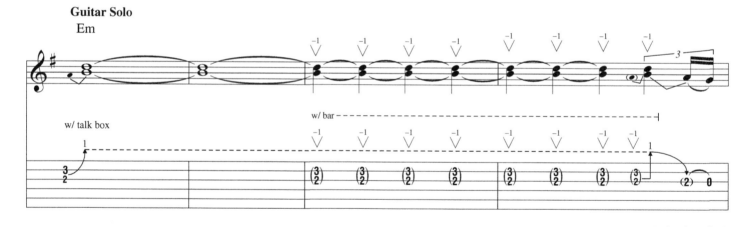

w/ talk box

w/ bar --------------------

D.S. al Coda 1
(take 2nd ending)

3. En -

talk box off   P.M. ----------   P.M.   P.M.   P.M.   P.M.   P.M. ----------

⊕ Coda 1

Chorus

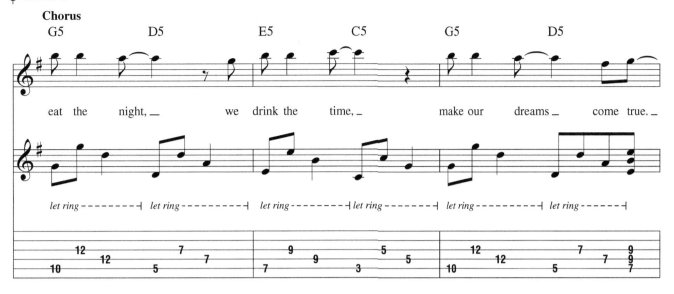

eat the night, ___ we drink the time, ___ make our dreams ___ come true. ___

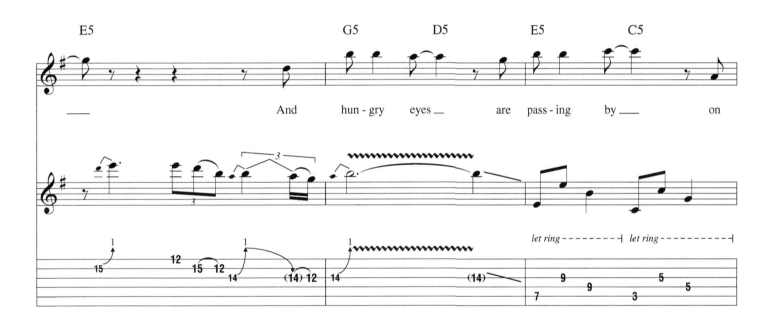

___ And hun - gry eyes ___ are pass - ing by ___ on

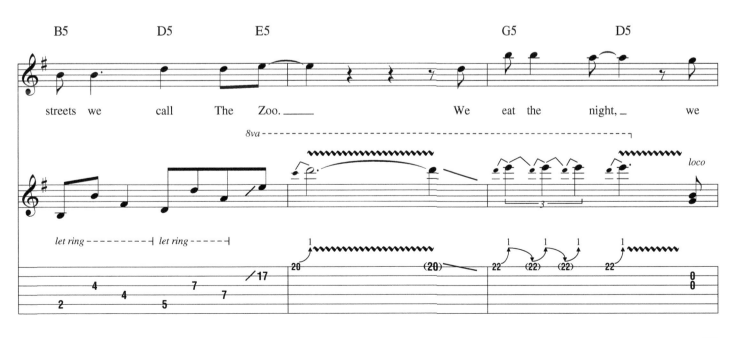

streets we call The Zoo. ___ We eat the night, ___ we

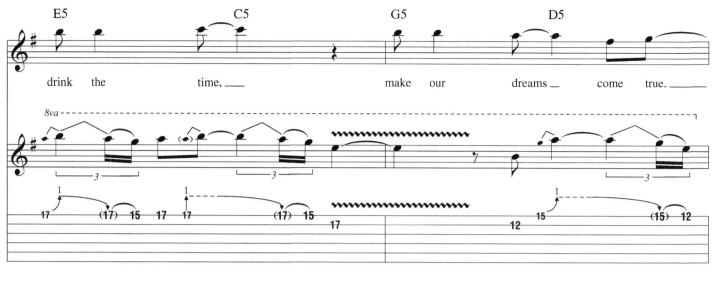

drink the   time, ___   make our   dreams ___ come true. ___

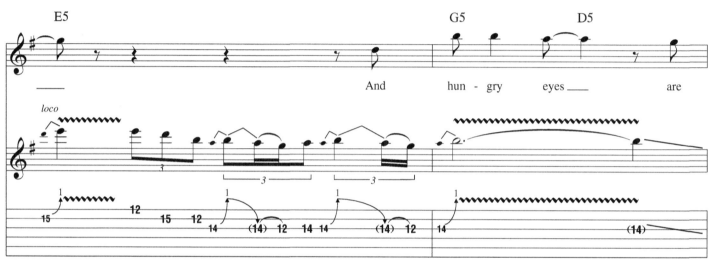

___   And   hun - gry   eyes ___   are

D.S.S. al Coda 2

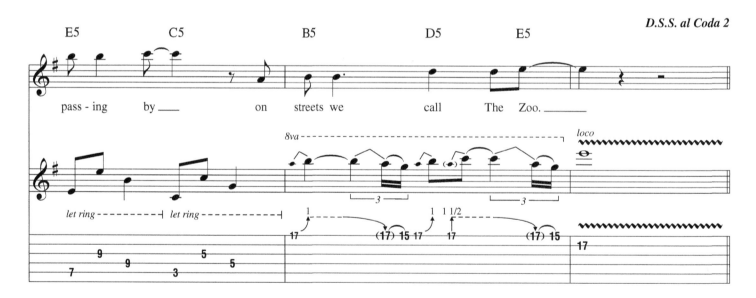

pass - ing   by ___   on   streets we   call   The Zoo. ___

 **Coda 2**

Outro-Guitar Solo

Em

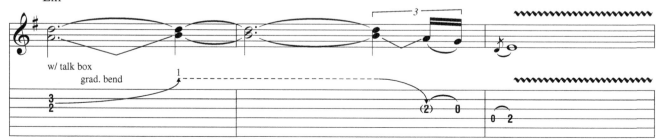

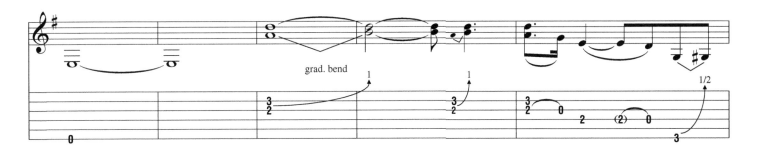

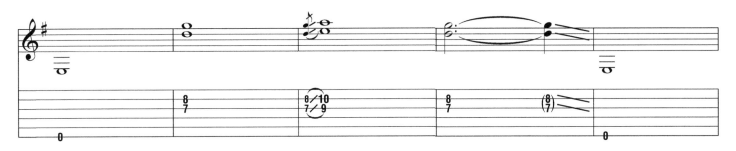

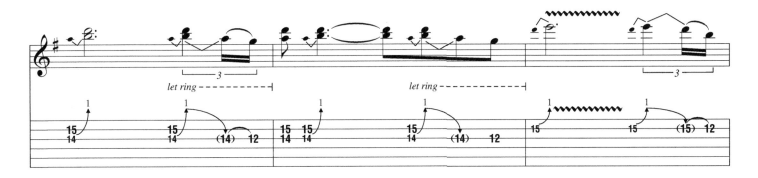

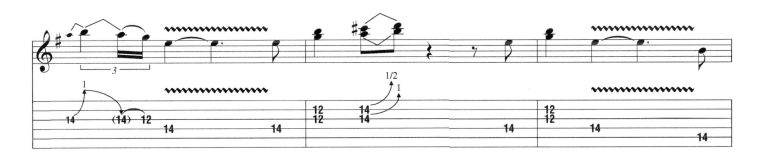

Begin fade   **Fade out**

Additional Lyrics

2. I meet my girl, she's dressed to kill.
   But all we gonna do
   Is walk around to catch the thrill
   On streets we call The Zoo.

3. Enjoy The Zoo and walk down
   42nd Street.
   Wanna be excited too,
   And you will feel the heat.

Rock You Like a Hurricane

Words and Music by Rudolf Schenker, Klaus Meine and Herman Rarebell

Intro

Moderate Rock ♩ = 124

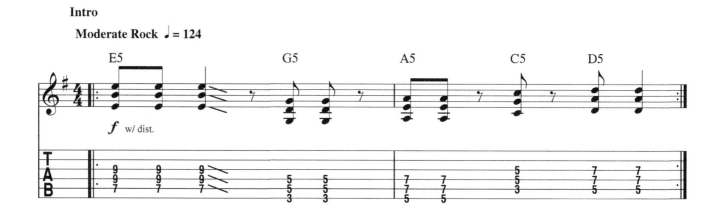

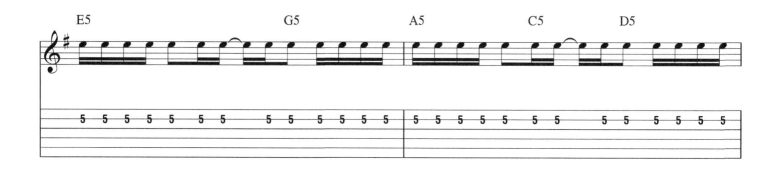

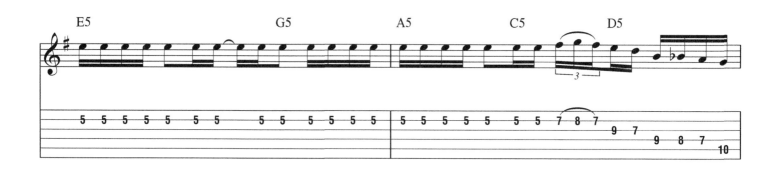

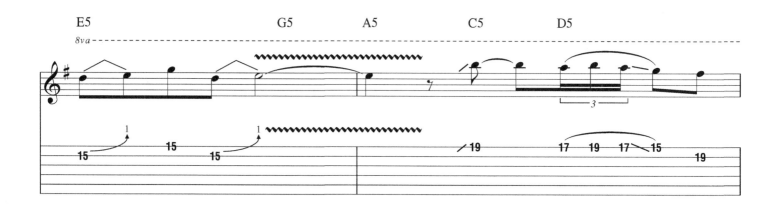

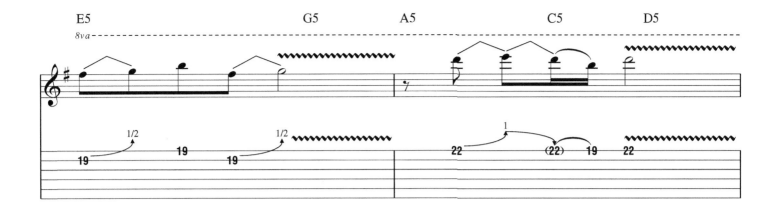

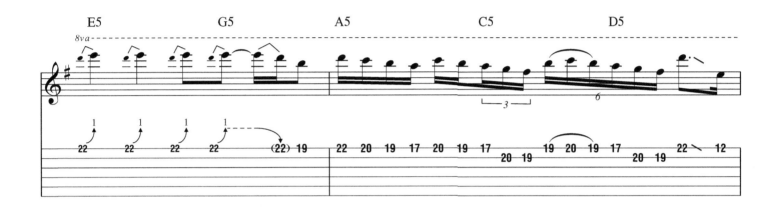

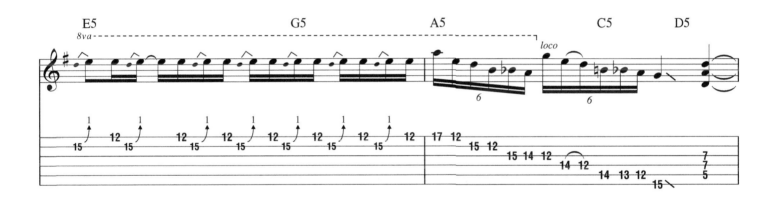

Verse

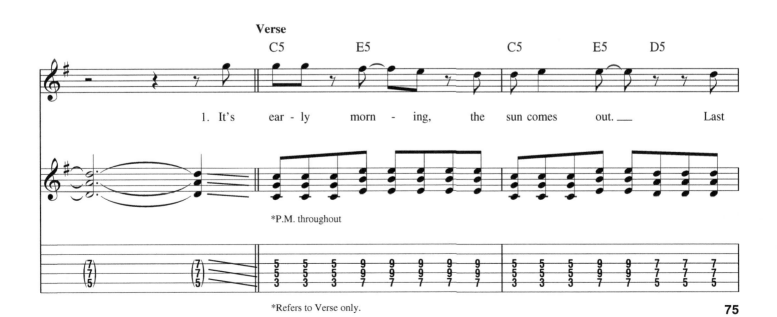

1. It's ear-ly morn-ing, the sun comes out. ___ Last

*P.M. throughout

*Refers to Verse only.

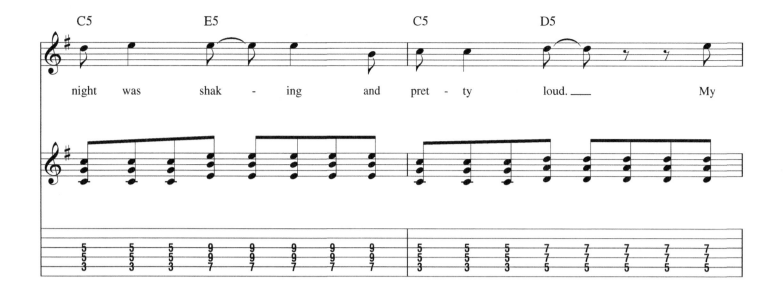

night was shak - ing and pret - ty loud. ___ My

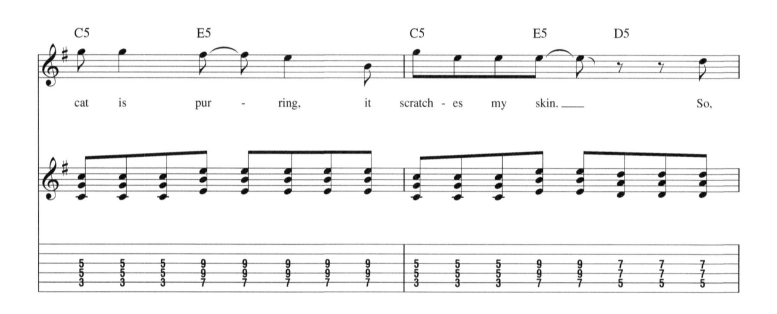

cat is pur - ring, it scratch - es my skin. ___ So,

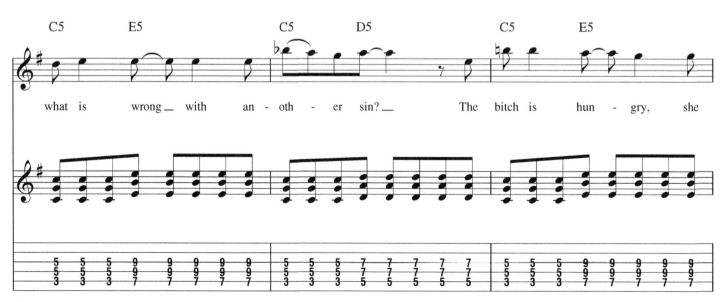

what is wrong __ with an - oth - er sin? __ The bitch is hun - gry, she

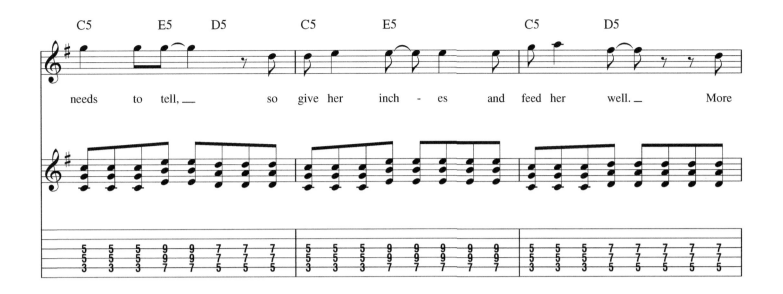

needs to tell, __ so give her inch - es and feed her well. __ More

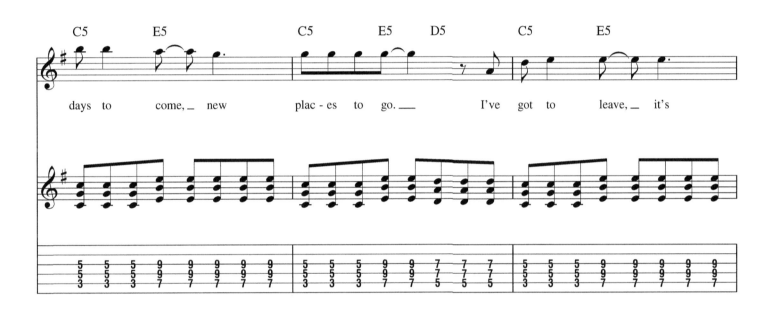

days to come, __ new plac - es to go. __ I've got to leave, __ it's

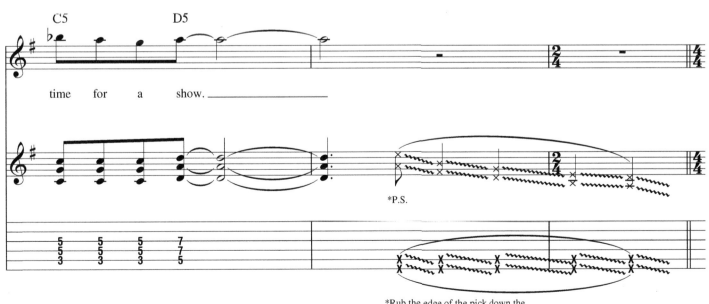

time for a show. _____

*P.S.

*Rub the edge of the pick down the
strings, producing a scratchy sound.

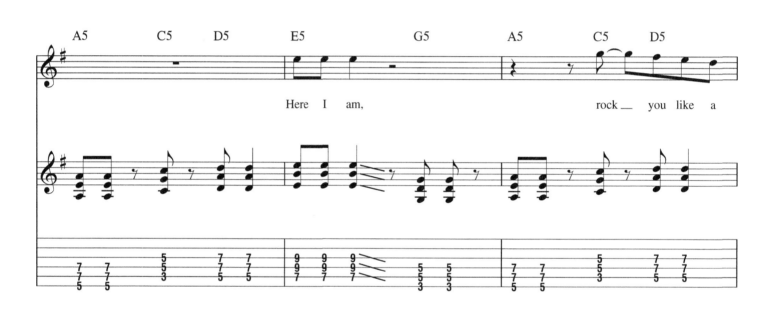

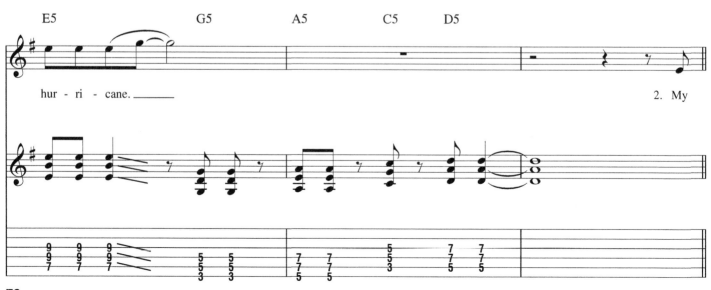

Verse
2nd time, Gtr. tacet, next 7 meas.

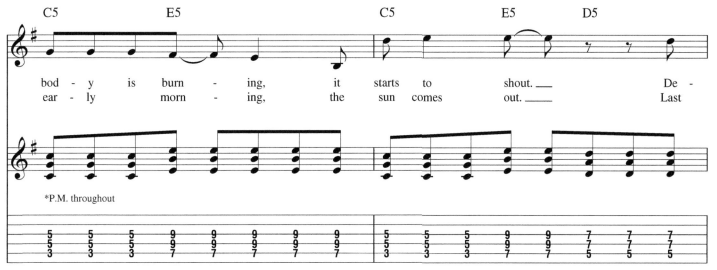

*P.M. throughout

*Refers to Verse only.

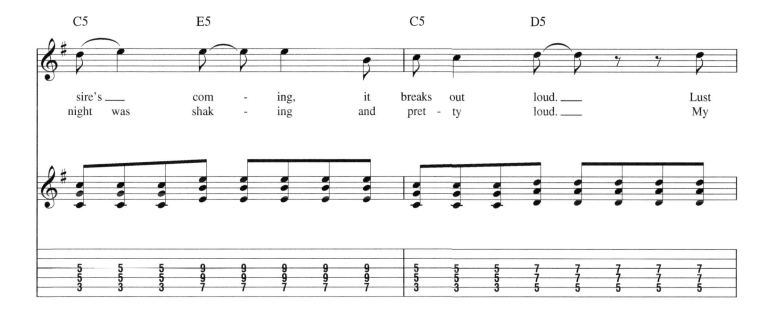

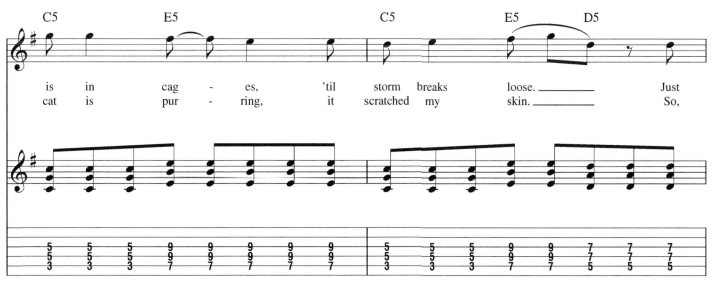

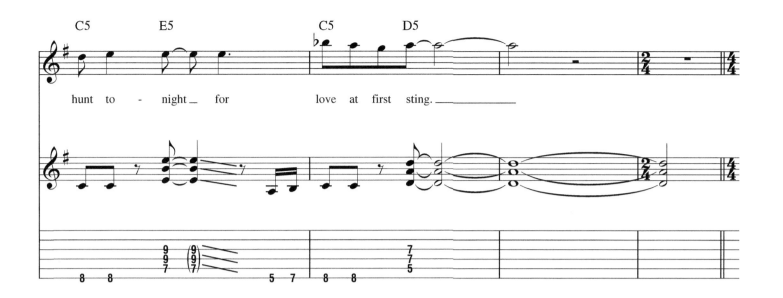

hunt to - night __ for love at first sting. _____

Chorus

Here I am, rock __ you like a hur - ri - cane.

To Coda ⊕

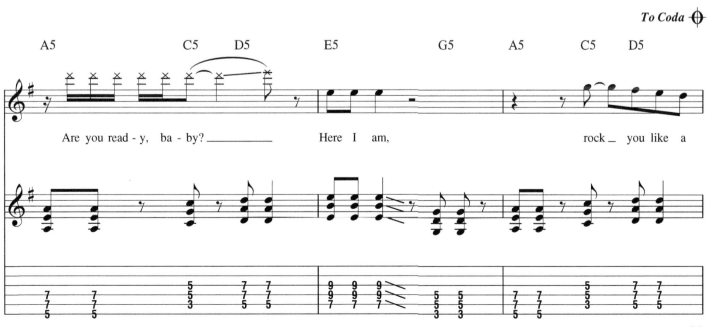

Are you read - y, ba - by? _____ Here I am, rock __ you like a

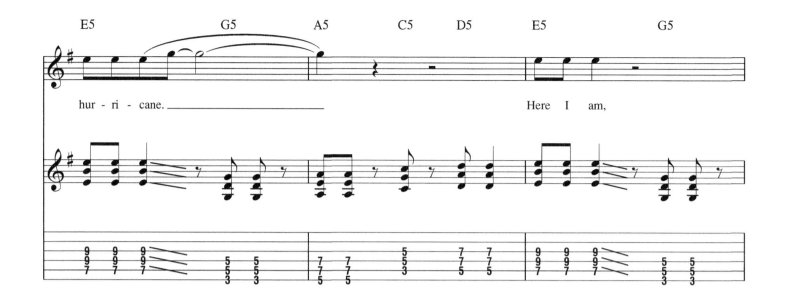

hur - ri - cane._____ Here I am,

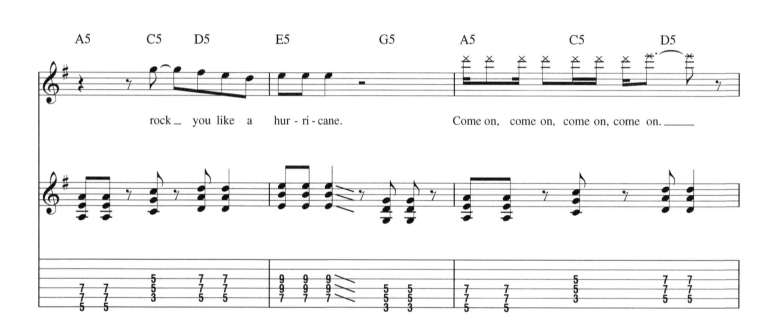

rock _ you like a hur - ri - cane. Come on, come on, come on, come on. ____

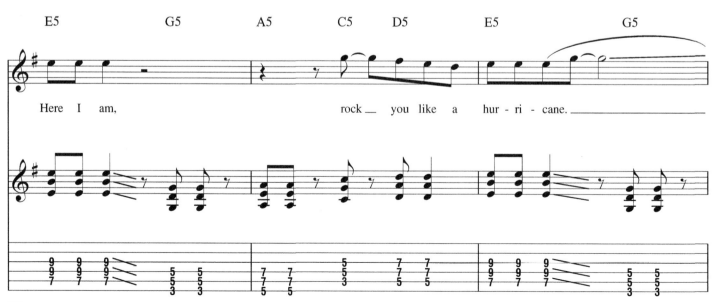

Here I am, rock _ you like a hur - ri - cane. _____

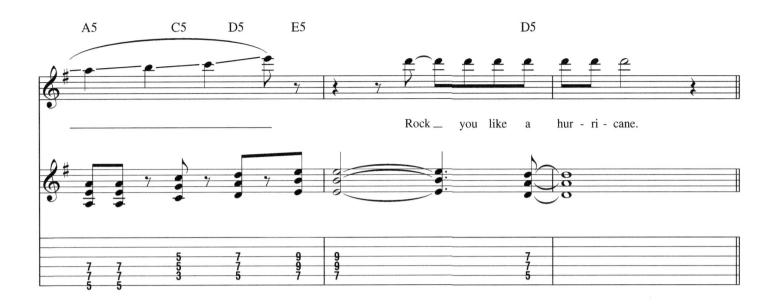

Rock — you like a hur - ri - cane.

Guitar Solo

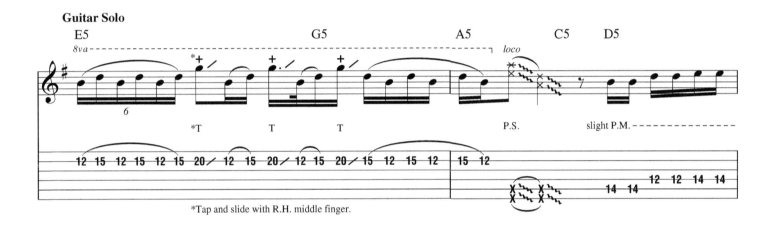

*Tap and slide with R.H. middle finger.

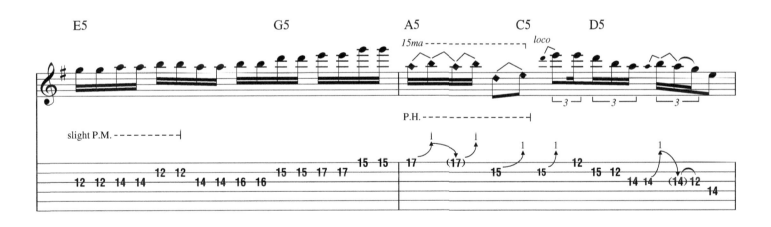

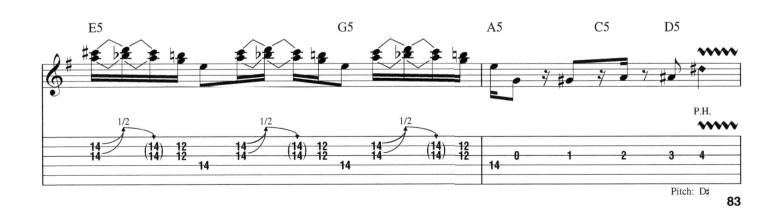

Pitch: D#

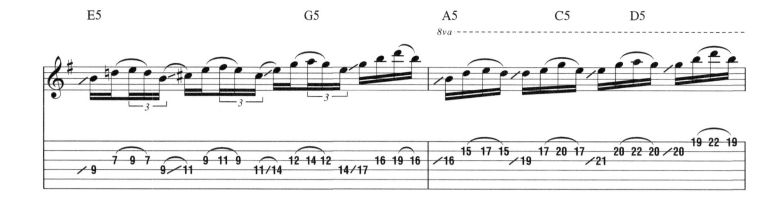

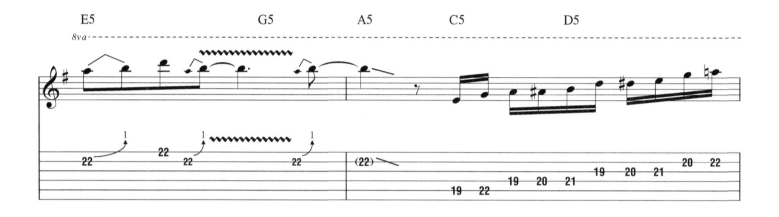

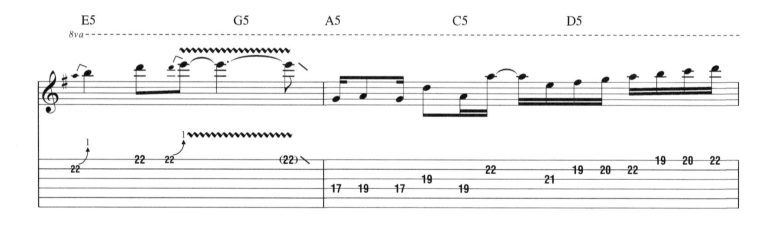

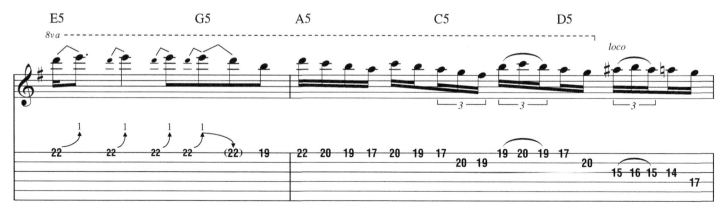

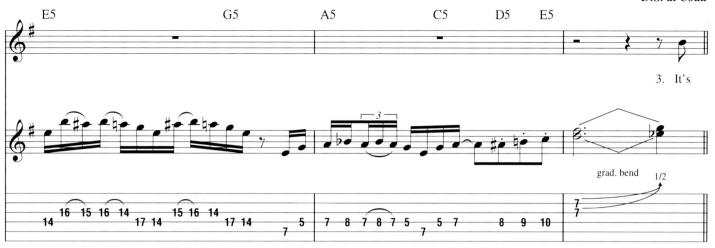

Coda

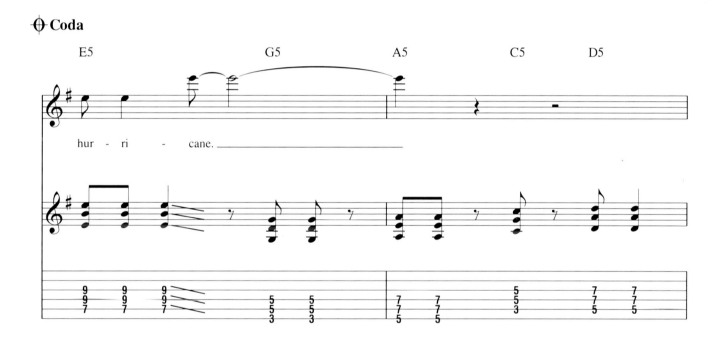

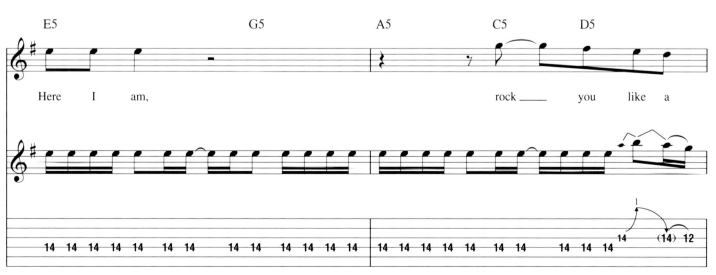

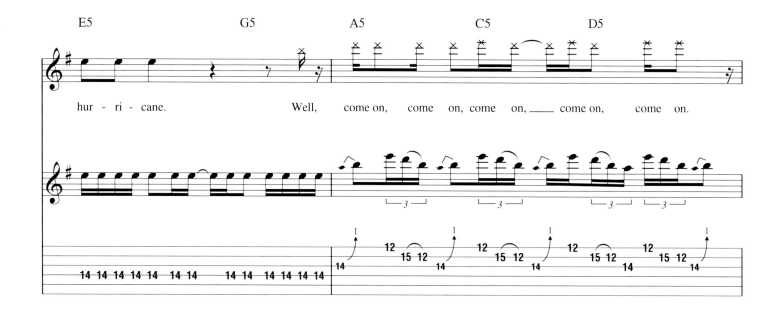

hur - ri - cane.   Well,   come on,   come on, come   on, ___ come on,   come on.

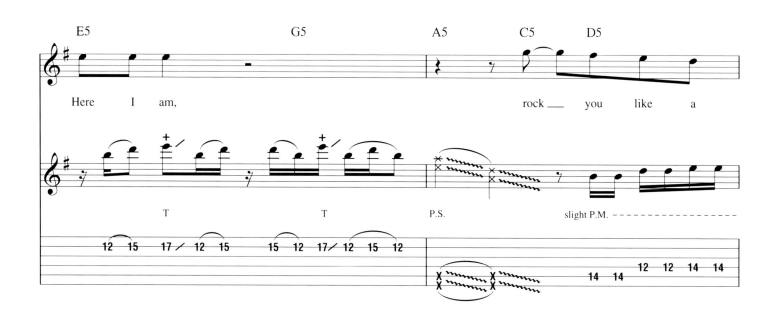

Here   I   am,   rock ___ you   like   a

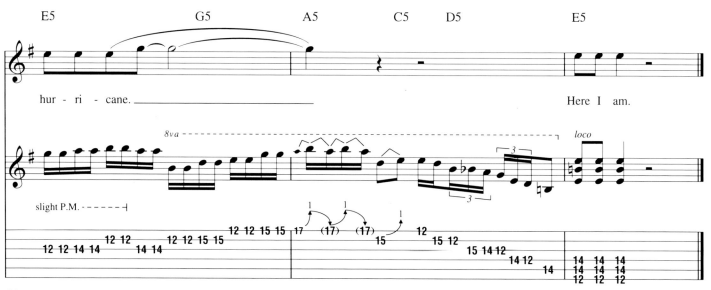

hur - ri - cane. _____   Here I am.

HAL•LEONARD® GUITAR PLAY-ALONG

INCLUDES TAB

AUDIO ACCESS INCLUDED

This series will help you play your favorite songs quickly and easily. Just follow the tab and listen to the audio to hear how the guitar should sound, and then play along using the separate backing tracks.

Playback tools are provided for slowing down the tempo without changing pitch and looping challenging parts. The melody and lyrics are included in the book so that you can sing or simply follow along.

 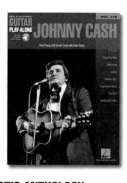

1. ROCK
00699570.................$16.99

2. ACOUSTIC
00699569.................$16.99

3. HARD ROCK
00699573.................$17.99

4. POP/ROCK
00699571.................$16.99

5. THREE CHORD SONGS
00300985.................$16.99

6. '90S ROCK
00298615.................$16.99

7. BLUES
00699575.................$17.99

8. ROCK
00699585.................$16.99

9. EASY ACOUSTIC SONGS
00151708.................$16.99

10. ACOUSTIC
00699586.................$16.95

11. EARLY ROCK
0699579.................$15.99

12. ROCK POP
00291724.................$16.99

14. BLUES ROCK
00699582.................$16.99

15. R&B
00699583.................$17.99

16. JAZZ
00699584.................$16.99

17. COUNTRY
00699588.................$16.99

18. ACOUSTIC ROCK
00699577.................$15.95

20. ROCKABILLY
00699580.................$16.99

21. SANTANA
00174525.................$17.99

22. CHRISTMAS
00699600.................$15.99

23. SURF
00699635.................$16.99

24. ERIC CLAPTON
00699649.................$17.99

25. THE BEATLES
00198265.................$17.99

26. ELVIS PRESLEY
00699643.................$16.99

27. DAVID LEE ROTH
00699645.................$16.95

28. GREG KOCH
00699646.................$17.99

29. BOB SEGER
00699647.................$16.99

30. KISS
00699644.................$16.99

32. THE OFFSPRING
00699653.................$14.95

33. ACOUSTIC CLASSICS
00699656.................$17.99

34. CLASSIC ROCK
00699658.................$17.99

35. HAIR METAL
00699660.................$17.99

36. SOUTHERN ROCK
00699661.................$19.99

37. ACOUSTIC UNPLUGGED
00699662.................$22.99

38. BLUES
00699663.................$17.99

39. '80S METAL
00699664.................$17.99

40. INCUBUS
00699668.................$17.95

41. ERIC CLAPTON
00699669.................$17.99

42. COVER BAND HITS
00211597.................$16.99

43. LYNYRD SKYNYRD
00699681.................$19.99

44. JAZZ GREATS
00699689.................$16.99

45. TV THEMES
00699718.................$14.95

46. MAINSTREAM ROCK
00699722.................$16.95

47. HENDRIX SMASH HITS
00699723.................$19.99

48. AEROSMITH CLASSICS
00699724.................$17.99

49. STEVIE RAY VAUGHAN
00699725.................$17.99

50. VAN HALEN 1978-1984
00110269.................$19.99

51. ALTERNATIVE '90S
00699727.................$14.99

52. FUNK
00699728.................$15.99

53. DISCO
00699729.................$14.99

54. HEAVY METAL
00699730.................$17.99

55. POP METAL
00699731.................$14.95

57. GUNS N' ROSES
00159922.................$17.99

58. BLINK-182
00699772.................$14.95

59. CHET ATKINS
00702347.................$16.99

60. 3 DOORS DOWN
00699774.................$14.95

62. CHRISTMAS CAROLS
00699798.................$12.95

63. CREEDENCE CLEARWATER REVIVAL
00699802.................$16.99

64. OZZY OSBOURNE
00699803.................$17.99

66. THE ROLLING STONES
00699807.................$17.99

67. BLACK SABBATH
00699808.................$16.99

68. PINK FLOYD – DARK SIDE OF THE MOON
00699809.................$17.99

71. CHRISTIAN ROCK
00699824.................$14.95

72. ACOUSTIC '90S
00699827.................$14.95

73. BLUESY ROCK
00699829.................$16.99

74. SIMPLE STRUMMING SONGS
00151706.................$19.99

75. TOM PETTY
00699882.................$19.99

76. COUNTRY HITS
00699884.................$16.99

77. BLUEGRASS
00699910.................$17.99

78. NIRVANA
00700132.................$16.99

79. NEIL YOUNG
00700133.................$24.99

80. ACOUSTIC ANTHOLOGY
00700175.................$19.95

81. ROCK ANTHOLOGY
00700176.................$22.99

82. EASY ROCK SONGS
00700177.................$17.99

84. STEELY DAN
00700200.................$19.99

85. THE POLICE
00700269.................$16.99

86. BOSTON
00700465.................$16.99

87. ACOUSTIC WOMEN
00700763.................$14.99

88. GRUNGE
00700467.................$16.99

89. REGGAE
00700468.................$15.99

90. CLASSICAL POP
00700469.................$14.99

91. BLUES INSTRUMENTALS
00700505.................$17.99

92. EARLY ROCK INSTRUMENTALS
00700506.................$15.99

93. ROCK INSTRUMENTALS
00700507.................$16.99

94. SLOW BLUES
00700508.................$16.99

95. BLUES CLASSICS
00700509.................$15.99

96. BEST COUNTRY HITS
00211615.................$16.99

97. CHRISTMAS CLASSICS
00236542.................$14.99

98. ROCK BAND
00700704.................$14.95

99. ZZ TOP
00700762.................$16.99

100. B.B. KING
00700466.................$16.99

101. SONGS FOR BEGINNERS
00701917.................$14.99

102. CLASSIC PUNK
00700769.................$14.99

103. SWITCHFOOT
00700773.................$16.99

104. DUANE ALLMAN
00700846.................$17.99

105. LATIN
00700939...................$16.99

106. WEEZER
00700958...................$14.99

107. CREAM
00701069...................$16.99

108. THE WHO
00701053...................$16.99

109. STEVE MILLER
00701054...................$19.99

110. SLIDE GUITAR HITS
00701055...................$16.99

111. JOHN MELLENCAMP
00701056...................$14.99

112. QUEEN
00701052...................$16.99

113. JIM CROCE
00701058...................$17.99

114. BON JOVI
00701060...................$16.99

115. JOHNNY CASH
00701070...................$16.99

116. THE VENTURES
00701124...................$17.99

117. BRAD PAISLEY
00701224...................$16.99

118. ERIC JOHNSON
00701353...................$16.99

119. AC/DC CLASSICS
00701356...................$17.99

120. PROGRESSIVE ROCK
00701457...................$14.99

121. U2
00701508...................$16.99

122. CROSBY, STILLS & NASH
00701610...................$16.99

123. LENNON & McCARTNEY ACOUSTIC
00701614...................$16.99

124. SMOOTH JAZZ
00200664...................$16.99

125. JEFF BECK
00701687...................$17.99

126. BOB MARLEY
00701701...................$17.99

127. 1970S ROCK
00701739...................$16.99

128. 1960S ROCK
00701740...................$14.99

129. MEGADETH
00701741...................$17.99

130. IRON MAIDEN
00701742...................$17.99

131. 1990S ROCK
00701743...................$14.99

132. COUNTRY ROCK
00701757...................$15.99

133. TAYLOR SWIFT
00701894...................$16.99

134. AVENGED SEVENFOLD
00701906...................$16.99

135. MINOR BLUES
00151350...................$17.99

136. GUITAR THEMES
00701922...................$14.99

137. IRISH TUNES
00701966...................$15.99

138. BLUEGRASS CLASSICS
00701967...................$17.99

139. GARY MOORE
00702370...................$16.99

140. MORE STEVIE RAY VAUGHAN
00702396...................$17.99

141. ACOUSTIC HITS
00702401...................$16.99

142. GEORGE HARRISON
00237697...................$17.99

143. SLASH
00702425...................$19.99

144. DJANGO REINHARDT
00702531...................$16.99

145. DEF LEPPARD
00702532...................$19.99

146. ROBERT JOHNSON
00702533...................$16.99

147. SIMON & GARFUNKEL
14041591...................$16.99

148. BOB DYLAN
14041592...................$16.99

149. AC/DC HITS
14041593...................$17.99

150. ZAKK WYLDE
02501717...................$19.99

151. J.S. BACH
02501730...................$16.99

152. JOE BONAMASSA
02501751...................$19.99

153. RED HOT CHILI PEPPERS
00702990...................$19.99

155. ERIC CLAPTON – FROM THE ALBUM UNPLUGGED
00703085...................$16.99

156. SLAYER
00703770...................$19.99

157. FLEETWOOD MAC
00101382...................$17.99

159. WES MONTGOMERY
00102593...................$19.99

160. T-BONE WALKER
00102641...................$17.99

161. THE EAGLES – ACOUSTIC
00102659...................$17.99

162. THE EAGLES HITS
00102667...................$17.99

163. PANTERA
00103036...................$17.99

164. VAN HALEN 1986-1995
00110270...................$17.99

165. GREEN DAY
00210343...................$17.99

166. MODERN BLUES
00700764...................$16.99

167. DREAM THEATER
00111938...................$24.99

168. KISS
00113421...................$17.99

169. TAYLOR SWIFT
00115982...................$16.99

170. THREE DAYS GRACE
00117337...................$16.99

171. JAMES BROWN
00117420...................$16.99

172. THE DOOBIE BROTHERS
00116970...................$16.99

173. TRANS-SIBERIAN ORCHESTRA
00119907...................$19.99

174. SCORPIONS
00122119...................$16.99

175. MICHAEL SCHENKER
00122127...................$17.99

176. BLUES BREAKERS WITH JOHN MAYALL & ERIC CLAPTON
00122132...................$19.99

177. ALBERT KING
00123271...................$16.99

178. JASON MRAZ
00124165...................$17.99

179. RAMONES
00127073...................$16.99

180. BRUNO MARS
00129706...................$16.99

181. JACK JOHNSON
00129854...................$16.99

182. SOUNDGARDEN
00138161...................$17.99

183. BUDDY GUY
00138240...................$17.99

184. KENNY WAYNE SHEPHERD
00138258...................$17.99

185. JOE SATRIANI
00139457...................$17.99

186. GRATEFUL DEAD
00139459...................$17.99

187. JOHN DENVER
00140839...................$17.99

188. MÖTLEY CRUE
00141145...................$17.99

189. JOHN MAYER
00144350...................$17.99

190. DEEP PURPLE
00146152...................$17.99

191. PINK FLOYD CLASSICS
00146164...................$17.99

192. JUDAS PRIEST
00151352...................$17.99

193. STEVE VAI
00156028...................$19.99

194. PEARL JAM
00157925...................$17.99

195. METALLICA: 1983-1988
00234291...................$19.99

196. METALLICA: 1991-2016
00234292...................$19.99

HAL•LEONARD®

For complete songlists, visit
Hal Leonard online at
www.halleonard.com

Prices, contents, and availability subject to
change without notice.
1120
9/12; 397